D0060450

TRANSFORMERS ARMADA™

THE UNICRON BATTLES

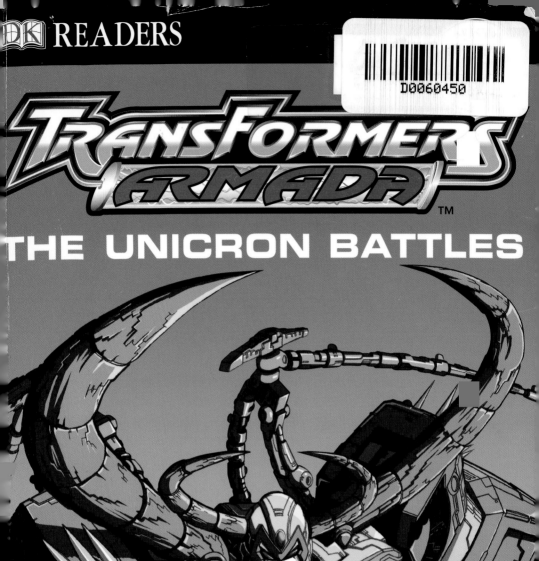

Andrew Donkin

DK READERS

Level 4

Days of the Knights

Volcanoes and Other Natural
 Disasters

Pirates: Raiders of the High
 Seas

Horse Heroes

Trojan Horse

Micro Monsters

Going for Gold!

Extreme Machines

Flying Ace: The Story of
 Amelia Earhart

Robin Hood

Black Beauty

Free at Last! The Story of
 Martin Luther King, Jr.

Joan of Arc

Spooky Spinechillers

Welcome to The Globe! The
 Story of Shakespeare's
 Theater

Antarctic Adventure

Space Station

Atlantis: The Lost City?

Dinosaur Detectives

Danger on the Mountain:
 Scaling the World's Highest
 Peaks

Crime Busters

The Story of Muhammad Ali

First Flight: The Story of the
 Wright Brothers

LEGO: Race for Survival

NFL: NFL's Greatest Upsets

NFL: Rumbling Running
 Backs

WCW: Going for Goldberg

WCW: Feel the Sting

MLB: Strikeout Kings

MLB: Super Shortstops: Jeter,
 Nomar, and A-Rod

MLB: The Story of the New
 York Yankees

JLA: Batman's Guide to Crime
 and Detection

JLA: Superman's Guide to the
 Universe

JLA: Wonder Woman's Book
 of Myths

JLA: Aquaman's Guide to the
 Oceans

The Story of the X-Men: How
 it all Began

Creating the X-Men: How
 Comic Books Come to Life

Spider-Man's Amazing Powers

The Story of Spider-Man

The Incredible Hulk's Book of
 Strength

The Story of the Incredible
 Hulk

Transformers Armada: The
 Awakening

Transformers Armada: The
 Quest

A Note to Parents

DK READERS is a compelling program for beginning readers, designed in conjunction with leading literacy experts.

Beautiful illustrations and superb full-color photographs combine with engaging, easy-to-read stories to offer a fresh approach to each subject in the series. Each DK READER is guaranteed to capture a child's interest while developing his or her reading skills, general knowledge, and love of reading.

The four levels of DK READERS are aimed at different reading abilities, enabling you to choose the books that are exactly right for your child:

Level 1 – Beginning to read
Level 2 – Beginning to read alone
Level 3 – Reading alone
Level 4 – Proficient readers

The "normal" age at which a child begins to read can be anywhere from three to eight years old, so these levels are only a general guideline.

No matter which level you select, you can be sure that you are helping your child learn to read, then read to learn!

LONDON, NEW YORK, MELBOURNE,
MUNICH, AND DELHI

Editor Kate Simkins
Designer Sooz Bellerby
Series Editor Alastair Dougall
Production Jenny Jacoby
Picture Researcher Bridget Tily

First American Edition, 2004
04 05 06 07 10 9 8 7 6 5 4 3 2
Published in the United States by DK Publishing, Inc.
375 Hudson Street, New York, New York 10014

Library of Congress Cataloging-in-Publication Data

Donkin, Andrew.
 Transformers Armada : the Unicron battles / by Andrew Donkin.-- 1st
American ed.
  p. cm. -- (DK readers)
Summary: While the Transformers battle Unicron together, Megatron still
longs to defeat Optimus Prime.
 ISBN 0-7566-0312-9 (PB) -- ISBN 0-7566-0313-7 (HC)
 [1. Science fiction.] I. Title: Unicron battles. II. Title. III.
Series: Dorling Kindersley readers.
 PZ7.D7175Ts 2004
 [Fic]--dc22
                        2003019546

Color reproduction by Colourscan, Singapore
Printed and bound in China by L Rex Printing Co., Ltd.

The publisher would like to thank the following for their kind permission
to reproduce their photographs:

a=above; c=center; b=below; l=left; r=right t=top;

18 Corbis: Joe McBride tl. 30 DK Images: Photo: Guy Ryecart cl. 32 DK
Images: London Planetarium tl. 33 Getty Images:
Steve Bloom cr. 38 Corbis: Michael S.Yamashita cl. 40 Ancient Art &
Architecture Collection: tl.

All other photographs © Dorling Kindersley.
For further information see: www.dkimages.com

Discover more at
www.dk.com

Contents

Robot power   4

Fighting as one   8

Origin   22

Mortal combat   36

Glossary   48

TM

The Unicron Battles

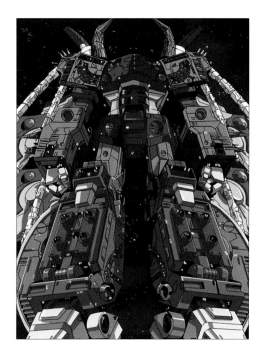

Written by Andrew Donkin

Robot power

Transformers are a race of giant alien robots from a distant world called Cybertron. All Transformers can change their robot form, becoming cars, planes, and tanks.

Long, long ago, the race of Transformers split into two groups—the peace-loving Autobots led by Optimus Prime and the evil, power-mad Decepticons led by Megatron, now known as Galvatron. The two factions have been fighting for control of Cybertron for millions of years.

Optimus Prime
The Autobot leader is the most respected of all the Autobots and has led them through countless battles against Galvatron and his Decepticons.

Optimus Prime and Galvatron are arch-enemies. They have fought many ferocious battles.

Megatron was a powerful fighting machine. He could transform into a missile tank.

Central to the conflict is a third race of smaller Transformers called Mini-Cons. Combining with a Mini-Con greatly increases the strength and firepower of the Autobots and Decepticons, making the little Mini-Cons the keys to victory in the war.

Knowing they were pawns in the Transformers' war, the Mini-Cons tried to escape from Cybertron. Their ship eventually crash-landed on Earth. Discovering the lost Mini-Cons' location, the Autobots and Decepticons raced across the galaxy to seek out the Mini-Cons.

Galvatron
Megatron changed his name to Galvatron after a power boost increased his strength. He is a dangerous and cunning warrior and is obsessed with becoming the sole ruler of Cybertron.

Galvatron is a self-centered bully. He uses his strength to overcome his friends and enemies alike.

The kids (clockwise from top left): Billy, Carlos, Alexis, Rad, and Fred.

Mini-Con team
The Mini-Cons Mirage, Dirt Boss, and Downshift are known as the Mini-Cons' Race Team.

Mirage

Now the battlefield has shifted once more. The warring Decepticons and Autobots (with their new human friends) have returned home to Cybertron only to discover that a far greater danger threatens them all.

Their new enemy is Unicron— an ancient evil older than even the Transformers. Upon their return, the traitor Thrust stole the most powerful Mini-Con weapons from under the nose of Galvatron.

Together with the mysterious Sideways, Thrust used the weapons to wake Unicron from his long hibernation.

The Transformers were shocked to learn that Cybertron's moon had been Unicron all along, just waiting to be woken up.

They also discovered the terrible truth about the Mini-Cons. They had been created by Unicron to deliberately intensify the Transformers' war.

Realizing the danger, Starscream sacrificed his own life to persuade Galvatron that he must join forces with his arch-enemy, Optimus Prime.

With Unicron's true form now fully revealed, can even the combined forces of the Transformers triumph against the greatest evil ever seen in the Universe?

Dirt Boss

Downshift

Unicron is a planet-sized mechanical robot. Unless the Transformers can stop him, he threatens to consume the planet of Cybertron piece by piece.

Special shield
The trio of Mirage, Dirt Boss, and Downshift also combine together to transform into the Skyboom Shield.

The spaceships of the Autobots and Decepticons assemble ready to attack Unicron.

Uneasy allies
The Autobots and the Decepticons had been enemies for millions of years, but the menace of Unicron has made Optimus Prime and Galvatron become uneasy allies. They exchanged an historical handshake as they united against Unicron.

Fighting as one

It was the largest space battle that the cosmos had ever seen. The space fleets of the Autobots and the Decepticons had combined to attack Unicron. However, the battle was not going well. The metal ring structure around Unicron's head crackled with a violent electric charge. Every time a Transformer ship flew in to attack, purple lightning flashed through space destroying craft after craft. The Transformers' fleet was taking heavy loses.

"All units retreat immediately!" ordered Galvatron.

From the surface of Unicron, Thrust was watching the battle.

"Fly away, you cowards!" he screamed in triumph at the fleeing armada.

Thrust had betrayed the entire Transformer race when he had helped Sideways wake Unicron. Now the mercenary was enjoying seeing the Transformers' fleet being blasted apart. As Unicron's new right-hand man, Thrust was looking forward with relish to helping him rule the Universe.

Chaos Bringer
Probably the largest living being in the entire cosmos, Unicron feeds by ripping whole planets apart and consuming them. He is known as the Chaos Bringer.

Thrust is delighted with the way things have turned out. By joining forces with Unicron, he now has all the power he ever wanted.

On the Autobot flagship, Optimus Prime was organizing the battle against Unicron.

"Galvatron and I are going to plan the strategy for our next attack," he said. "Hoist, you keep analyzing the data from the Autobot probes and see if you can find a weak spot on Unicron."

"I've done a full scan of Unicron's entire structure, sir," reported Hoist. "So far, nothing, but I'll keep looking."

Then the gathered Transformers let out a gasp as they saw that Unicron was on the move again.

"He's got a new target— Cybertron itself! Come on!" shouted Hot Shot. "We have to save Cybertron."

Hot Shot and Wheeljack go on a daring mission to save their planet from annihilation.

A few minutes later, Hot Shot and Wheeljack were speeding toward Unicron in two Discovery Pods. Although they were no match for Unicron, Hot Shot was determined to save their home world…whatever the price.

"Careful, it's going to get pretty hairy out there. Stay close to my wing, okay, Wheeljack!" said Hot Shot.

The two pods swooped toward Unicron with all guns blazing.

Wheeljack
Although he is a Decepticon, Wheeljack was good friends with Hot Shot many years ago before the war started. He is delighted to find himself fighting alongside his old friend once more.

Rad, Carlos, Alexis, Fred, and Billy watched the attack from the relative safety of the Autobot flagship.

"Hot Shot's lasers aren't even making a mark on Unicron!" said Alexis, worried for her friend's life.

"If they're not careful, they're gonna get squashed for sure!" said Fred, half closing his eyes.

Then, as Hot Shot and Wheeljack flew in low across the surface of Unicron's body, they saw something that neither of them had expected.

"Look, there's that weasel Thrust. I say we take him out!" shouted Wheeljack.

"All units, direct your fire at Thrust!" ordered Hot Shot.

Evil one
Unicron's exact origins are lost in the mists of time. Ancient Cybertron legends describe how Unicron and his twin brother, Primus, are nearly as old as the Universe itself.

Immediately, Thrust's hiding place was attacked by a barrage of purple light bullets, making him run for his life.

"Something's happening on Unicron's chest. He's getting ready to blast Cybertron again!" said Hot Shot in alarm.

Suddenly an energy beam burst from Unicron's chest, blasting part of Cybertron into rubble. Unicron sucked up the debris into a hole in his chest—the planet-eater was feeding!

Planet-eater
Unicron has two forms— one a massive, moon-sized battle fortress bristling with weapons, and the other a goliath-sized robot.

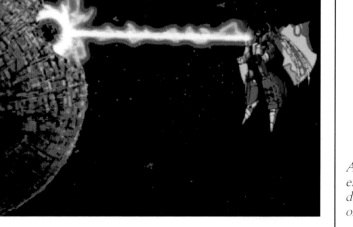

A powerful beam of energy from Unicron does great damage on Cybertron.

Jetstorm

Team work
Jetstorm, Runway, and Sonar are three very special Mini-Cons. They can combine to form another of the three mighty Mini-Con weapons, the Star Saber, a bright blue sword.

Optimus explains his plan to save Cybertron.

As the planet-eater continued his attack on the Transformers' home world, Optimus Prime laid out his plan to save Cybertron.

"The fleet will engage Unicron in battle, aiming all fire at a weak spot on his neck that Hoist has discovered. But I don't think we're going to beat Unicron from the outside," said the Autobot leader.

"What do you mean?" asked Carlos in surprise.

"It was the Mini-Con weapons that Thrust stole that woke him up—the Requiem Blaster, the Skyboom Shield, and the Star Saber. If we can rescue those Mini-Cons from inside Unicron, maybe we can weaken him enough to give the fleet a chance," said Optimus.

"Great idea, Optimus, but how are you going to do it?" asked Rad.

"Galvatron and I are going to have to voyage *inside* Unicron," he said, to stunned silence.

Under Hot Shot's command, the fleet moved forward to begin their attack. Hundreds of Autobot and Decepticon ships surged through space in a perfect attack pattern. Win or lose, this was going to be the Transformers' biggest test.

Runway

Secret weapons
Thrust used the Star Saber, the Skyboom Shield, and the Requiem Blaster to wake up the sleeping Unicron.

Sonar

Optimus Prime and Galvatron combined with their Mini-Cons ready for battle.

"Transform!" shouted Optimus, powerlinking with Jetfire.

The two leaders dodged through the laser fire and dived toward Unicron.

Optimus Prime powerlinks with Jetfire to boost his firepower.

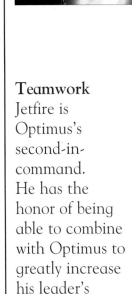

"Head for the vent right above that plasma burst," suggested Galvatron.

As Galvatron flew closer, he saw a familiar figure standing on Unicron's surface.

"Thrust! You traitorous worm! You dared to betray me," shouted Galvatron with fury.

Thrust leaped into the air to escape, but as he did so, he smashed into one of Unicron's weapon systems. The traitor crashed back violently onto Unicron's surface.

Teamwork
Jetfire is Optimus's second-in-command. He has the honor of being able to combine with Optimus to greatly increase his leader's strength.

He landed in the gap between two of Unicron's mighty panels just as they were closing. Thrust's eyes bulged with pain—his own master was accidentally crushing him to death.

"Galvatron! You can't leave me here! Please save me!" pleaded Thrust in desperation.

"If you dare to dream of such power, Thrust, do not be surprised if you are consumed by it," said Galvatron, coldly.

Seconds later, the double-crosser Thrust was non-operational.

Thrust
This sneaky Decepticon is an utterly evil Transformer. He betrayed his entire race when Unicron became his new master. Thrust cares only for himself and for power.

Galvatron has no mercy for the traitor Thrust.

Free falling
Also known as skydiving, free falling is when a person or group jumps from an aircraft and drops through the air. At around 2,000 feet (600 meters) above the ground, the skydivers must open their parachutes.

Unicron had broken through the defense shield Hot Shot had created to delay him and was feeding again.

The beam of bright, white energy that poured out of Unicron's chest was breaking Cybertron down, ready to be eaten. The energy beam suddenly vanished and Unicron created a vortex, drawing the pieces of planet debris into an opening in his body.

Optimus Prime and Galvatron were watching closely from their hiding place on Unicron's surface. They knew it was time for them to make their move.

"Are you ready, Galvatron?"

"I am," answered the Decepticon leader. Optimus and Galvatron jumped into space.

They allowed themselves to free-fall into the path of the wreckage.

As they joined the stream of rubble, they were sucked inside Unicron with the rest of the debris.

The huge metal grids on Unicron's chest slammed shut as his feeding frenzy came to an end. Optimus Prime and Galvatron realized they were now trapped inside his body! Would they be able to save Cybertron?

Optimus Prime and Galvatron float into Unicron among the pieces of Cybertron.

Feeding tube
Unicron feeds by sucking planets into a hole in his chest. When you eat, your food goes via your mouth into a long tube called the digestive system.

The Transformer leaders have traveled into the center of Unicron. They hope to defeat the planet-eater from the inside.

High Wire tells the kids that he might have a way of defeating Unicron.

Human friends
The kids first became involved in the Transformers' struggles after Rad and Carlos discovered several Mini-Cons hiding inside a mountain cave.

Rad and his friends had been watching the action from the Autobot flagship.

"I hope those two know what they're doing," said Rad, shaking his head.

High Wire, Rad's own Mini-Con, had just learned of Optimus Prime's plan and was looking very worried.

"Rad, I don't think Optimus's idea will work. When those Mini-Cons were placed inside Unicron, he took over their conscious minds. Only another Mini-Con would have any chance of waking them! I have to go inside!" explained High Wire.

"If that's the only way," said Rad, "then we're going in with you. After all, we didn't come all the way to Cybertron just to be spectators. Our friends are fighting for their lives and we need to help! We have to get inside Unicron!"

"But how can we possibly get in there? We couldn't survive being sucked in like Optimus and Galvatron," said Alexis.

"Use the underground warp gate on Cybertron," said Red Alert. "Hurry, you might be our last hope!"

Skilled officer
Red Alert is the Autobots' science officer and medic. He also acts as their mechanic, using his special skills to help repair any injuries to the team.

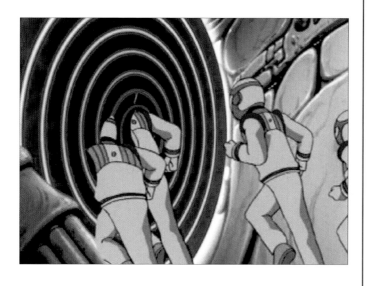

The warp gate on Cybertron takes the kids inside Unicron.

The kids and their Mini-Con friends rush to help Optimus and Galvatron.

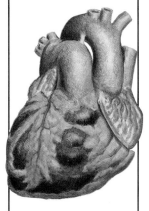

Big pump
Like Unicron's heart, the human heart beats. This is because the human heart pumps blood around the body. During an average lifetime, a human heart will beat around 2,000 million times.

Origin

The five kids, along with High Wire, Sureshock, and Grindor raced to the underground warp tunnel and just made it through before the tunnel collapsed.

"That was too close for comfort!" said Rad, as he and his friends emerged from the warp gate and found themselves inside Unicron.

They knew there was no going back. They would find a way to beat Unicron, or they would die.

"Come on, we've got to find Optimus and Galvatron," said Rad, and the group raced off.

Deep inside, Optimus and Galvatron stepped into the central chamber and found themselves staring at Unicron's giant heart.

"Look, there's the Star Saber and the other Mini-Con weapons," said Galvatron, moving forward.

Suddenly a mass of thrashing tentacles appeared from the floor of the cave, blocking Galvatron's path.

"We've got to watch our step," said Optimus quickly. "Unicron's entire body is like a giant booby trap! One wrong move, and we're dead!"

Galvatron and Optimus travel deep inside Unicron to the central chamber. There they discover Unicron's massive, beating heart.

Long arms
Unicron uses his tentacles like arms to hold onto Optimus and Galvatron. An octopus also has tentacles that it uses to grasp onto its prey. All octopuses have eight tentacles. Each one has two rows of suckers on its underside.

Unicron's heart is powered by the Mini-Con weapons: the Star Saber, the Skyboom Shield, and the Requiem Blaster.

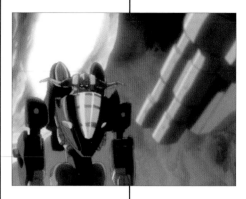

Sideways appears inside Unicron. He tells Optimus Prime and Galvatron the terrible truth about their battles.

Secret agent
Optimus Prime and Galvatron were shocked to learn that Sideways wasn't really another Transformer after all. He was part of Unicron, disguised as a separate being.

Unicron's core suddenly gave off a blinding white flash, and a figure materialized in the light.

"Sideways!" exclaimed Optimus. "You've been working with Unicron all along, haven't you?"

"Actually, we are one and the same. This shell you've come to know as Sideways is just a disguise. For eons, I've absorbed energy from your war. The war that I started and planned so I could feed on your hate!" laughed Sideways smugly.

Optimus and Galvatron were both too shocked to speak. They just stared in horror.

"Tell me, Optimus, why did you waste so much time fighting with Galvatron?" asked Sideways.

"I was fighting for peace!" said Optimus firmly.

"How foolish! To battle in the name of peace! How absurd!" observed Sideways, smirking with pleasure at Optimus's discomfort.

"You're beginning to get on my nerves, you overgrown garbage can," screamed Galvatron, preparing to attack Sideways.

But before Galvatron or Optimus could move, a mass of purple tentacles enveloped both of them. The snakelike tentacles tightened their hold, and the two mighty warriors knew that they were utterly helpless.

Double-crosser
Unicron created the identity of Sideways to help ensure that the war between the Autobots and the Decepticons continued.

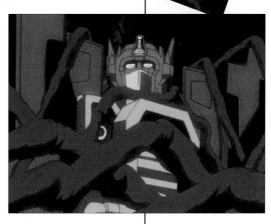

Unicron's powerful tentacles imprison Optimus and Galvatron.

Safety in numbers
An armada is a group of sea or space vessels sailing together. Vessels travel in a group on long voyages to keep each other safe.

Outside in space, it looked like Hot Shot's squad had made some progress at last. One of the bombing raids on Unicron's neck had broken through his strong armor plating.

Hot Shot led his six-plane squad through the jagged hole in Unicron's outer armor. The ships sped through tunnel after tunnel, flying deep into Unicron's interior. Finally, Hot Shot gave the order to fire on the giant robot.

"Okay, men, drop bombs!" shouted Hot Shot.

The ships dropped their lethal payloads of blast bombs.

The massed ranks of the Transformers' ships get ready to drop their bombs on the mighty Unicron.

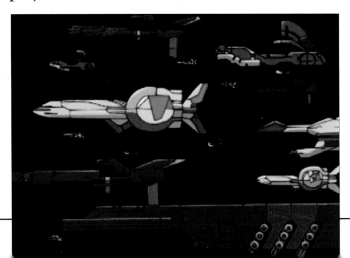

Unicron takes a direct hit, but he is able to repair the damage instantly.

"BOOM!"

As huge flames spread through Unicron's interior, the ships turned tail and raced for the exit.

"Yeah, baby!" said Hot Shot as he watched the smoke pouring out of Unicron. Then, quite suddenly, the damaged surface of Unicron's armor rippled. With horror, Hot Shot realized that Unicron was able to instantly repair himself!

"Your minions outside may think they are wearing me down, Optimus, but their attacks are only feeding me— making me even stronger!" boasted Unicron.

Trusted friend
Hot Shot's Mini-Con partner is Jolt. He has helped save Hot Shot from many dangerous situations.

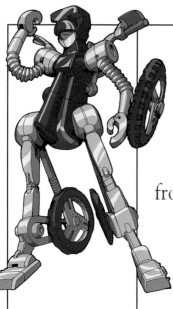

High Wire
This Mini-Con transforms from robot mode to become a fast-moving bike. His human partner is Rad, and there is a strong bond between them.

The kids are astonished to find Optimus and Galvatron trapped inside Unicron.

"Admit it, Optimus," said Sideways. "You actually enjoyed all the fighting with Galvatron!"

"That's not true!" said a voice from the other side of the chamber.

"Looks like your fan club has arrived, Optimus," said Sideways with a smirk.

The kids and the three Mini-Cons had found their way to the central chamber.

"Not everyone enjoys war like you, you metal moron," shouted Carlos crossly.

"Yeah, the Mini-Cons were programmed for peace," said Alexis.

"You humans know nothing of these matters," scoffed Sideways.

"You are wrong. We were programmed for peace, and we will fight for it!" said High Wire defiantly.

The kids' three Mini-Cons began to advance menacingly toward Sideways.

"Your confidence is misguided," said Sideways. "Unicron is more powerful than you."

Outside in space, the Mini-Cons had combined to try to keep Unicron away from Cybertron. Using their special powers, they had changed into a glowing green version of Unicron himself. Now, however, they started moving apart. Something big was happening.

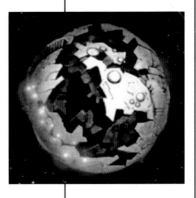

Broken planet
The planet Cybertron has paid a great price for the Autobot-Decepticon war. Its once-mighty metal cities now lie in ruins. It will take all the Transformers' energy to repair their shattered home world.

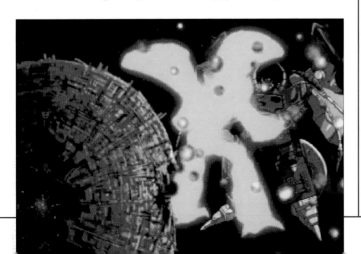

The Mini-Cons try to save Cybertron by becoming a mass of glowing green energy, shaped like Unicron himself.

The Mini-Cons fall under Unicron's mind control.

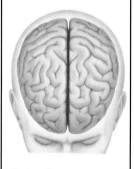

Mind matters
The mind is where thoughts come from. It is the same as the brain, which contains over 100 billion interlinked nerve cells.

Tentacles from Unicron wrap themselves around Rad. He and the other kids' minds are now linked with Unicron.

The Mini-Cons were attacking Unicron, but as they came closer to him, each and every one of them fell under his control.

"Welcome home, my Mini-Cons!" said Unicron's voice, booming in triumph.

Rad realized what was happening, but it was too late. Tentacles sprang from the floor and completely enveloped the kids. As they blacked out, each of the kids' consciousness was consumed into Unicron's mind, just like the Mini-Cons' before them.

What happened next was the weirdest experience of Rad's life.

When he woke up, Rad seemed to be back in his own home for a second. Then, just like in a dream, he found himself in a hot desert surrounded by his friends. After a few seconds, the scene changed again, and he saw Galvatron sitting on a throne. All the kids were having the same dream.

"I get it. We've mindlinked with Unicron—just as the Mini-Cons and Galvatron have. What we are seeing is one of Galvatron's fantasies!" explained Alexis.

Dry place
A desert is an area without enough rain to support human life. About one third of Earth's land surface is desert.

Galvatron's dream shows him sitting on a throne as Master of the Universe.

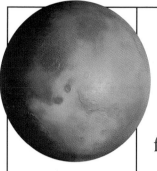

Rock in space
Like the bleak planet the kids find themselves on, Mars is a rocky planet. It is most famous for its red color. Mars is the fourth planet from the Sun.

Without warning, the scene changed again, and the friends found themselves in a beautiful forest clearing.

Alexis had used the power of her mind to create her own fantasy.

"That's so cool!" said Rad, impressed by his friend's quick thinking and intelligence.

The kids suddenly got a flash of a pair of terrifying blood-red eyes watching them. It was Unicron cutting into their mind fantasy.

"If we're all linked, maybe we can wake up the Mini-Cons," said Rad.

The kids started calling out to their Mini-Con friends.

Alexis makes up her own fantasy world, and the kids find themselves in a beautiful forest.

"High Wire! You've gotta wake up!" shouted the kids.

The scene changed once again and the youngsters found themselves on a bleak, rocky planet. The ground shook beneath their feet as a whirlwind started to suck up rocks and boulders.

Unicron's evil eyes stare menacingly at the kids.

"My patience has run out," said Unicron. "It is time to end this foolishness. Time to destroy you!"

The kids screamed in terror, realizing they were facing almost certain annihilation.

"High Wire, help us!" shouted Rad, in desperation.

Twister
A whirlwind is a rotating storm, also called a tornado or twister. Large whirlwinds can do great damage to property.

On the desolate, rocky planet, the kids face destruction by the evil Unicron.

Balls of green energy fill the bright blue sky as the Mini-Cons break free of Unicron's power.

Short circuits
Many machines that run on electricity contain circuit boards. These change the current of electricity into a form that can be used by the machine.

There was another flash of bright, white light, and the kids were stunned to find themselves standing under a perfect blue sky. The sky itself was crowded with hundreds and hundreds of green balls of Mini-Con energy.

"What!?" snarled Unicron.

Somehow the Mini-Cons had heard Rad's appeal for help. His friendship with High Wire had been strong enough to enable the Mini-Con to break free from Unicron's control, and he had awoken the rest of his race.

Now that the Mini-Cons were thinking for themselves again, what they wanted more than anything was peace, even if they had to fight Unicron to get it.

"You will pay for this!" said Unicron angrily.

But Unicron was already too late. Outside in space the Mini-Con fleet suddenly bombarded the massive body of Unicron with energy. The Mini-Cons were part of Unicron, and their attack was devastating. Every unit on his body began to short circuit.

Full of energy
There are many different kinds of energy—electrical, nuclear, and chemical, as well as light, sound, and heat. A flame has both light and heat.

Because they are part of him, Unicron has no defense against the Mini-Cons' attack.

Optimus's dilemma
Being leader of the Autobots has sometimes meant that Optimus has to make very difficult decisions. Should he carry on the fight with Galvatron?

Mortal combat

Inside Unicron's core, the Mini-Con weapons were released, and the tentacles holding the bodies of Optimus, Galvatron, and the kids suddenly withered and died.

"We're free!" said Rad.

In the central chamber, Sideways realized what had happened and wanted revenge. He leaped forward to attack Rad and the Mini-Cons, but Optimus blasted him to pieces. His smoking remains lay scattered across the floor.

They had won!

Unicron is finally defeated by the power of the Mini-Cons.

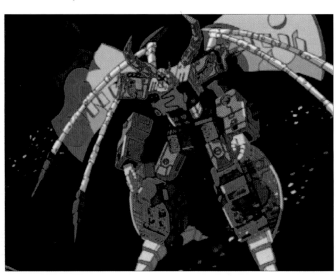

The battle was over.
Sideways was disabled, and
Unicron had been defeated.
But if Optimus imagined that
his troubles were over, he was wrong.
There was still someone around with
an old score to settle.

"You didn't expect us to *remain*
allies after Unicron was destroyed,
did you?" shouted Galvatron. "If we
don't continue our battle, then
everything we've done in the past
will have been pointless. Our fight
will carry on until one of us falls!"

The kids could hardly believe
their ears. Even after all the fighting,
Galvatron still wanted to finish his
war with Optimus.

Final conflict
Although he
has helped to
defeat Unicron,
Galvatron still
craves one final
victory over
Optimus Prime.
Will it be
Galvatron's
undoing?

*The kids can't
believe that
Galvatron wants
to keep fighting
Optimus.*

Rad tries to persuade Optimus not to fight Galvatron again.

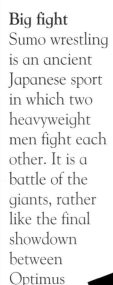

Big fight
Sumo wrestling is an ancient Japanese sport in which two heavyweight men fight each other. It is a battle of the giants, rather like the final showdown between Optimus and the evil Galvatron.

"The only way to destroy Unicron forever is to finish what I started and end the Autobot-Decepticon war for good!" explained Optimus.

"No, Optimus," called Rad. "Don't let him suck you into this! You don't have to fight!"

Rad's words came too late. Optimus had made up his mind.

Optimus leaped across the chamber bringing his fists smashing down into Galvatron. Both Transformers crashed to the floor and then spun quickly around, ready to try and land the next blow.

After Unicron's defeat, Optimus and Galvatron resume their titanic battle.

Meanwhile, back at the Transformers' base, Hot Shot heard that Optimus and Galvatron were facing off one last time. Some of his men had reported seeing slight movement in the supposedly dead Unicron. Would Unicron be able to feed on the energy from their battle and come alive again?

Inside Unicron, Galvatron and Optimus were fighting as never before. The two leaders rushed toward each other. Optimus reached out and ripped away part of Galvatron's shoulder armor.

Battle dress
Medieval knights wore suits of armor to protect them on the battlefield. Their suits were made of interlocking steel plates, not unlike the armor of Optimus and Galvatron.

Galvatron is struck a mighty blow by Optimus Prime.

Great battle
Optimus's and Galvatron's last battle was a mighty struggle. Ancient legends tell of many amazing fights, such as the combat between Hector, prince of Troy, and Achilles, champion of the Greeks. Achilles was the victor.

Galvatron got up and aimed his gun at Optimus. With brilliant aim, Optimus threw a piece of metal into the gun barrel. When Galvatron pulled the trigger, the gun exploded, blasting him through the chamber wall.

Recovering quickly, Galvatron lifted Optimus Prime off the floor, smashing his head into the chamber's ceiling and then shocking him with a high-voltage energy beam. As they fought, the warriors crashed through another wall.

Galvatron and Optimus Prime are well matched. Their final battle is long and ferocious.

They suddenly found themselves on the exterior surface of Unicron, staring out into space.

Both robots were exhausted.

"This can't be how our fight ends, Prime! I demand satisfaction! Get up so I can destroy you!" screamed Galvatron.

Optimus slowly struggled to his feet and squared up to his enemy.

As the conflict was about the start again, Hot Shot and his battle squad spotted Optimus and Galvatron on Unicron's surface.

"Your fighting is bringing Unicron back to life!" shouted Hot Shot, worried for his leader's life.

Deadly tank
In vehicle mode, Galvatron becomes a powerful super-tank, truly a deadly foe on any battlefield. Galvatron's Mini-Con partner is Clench.

Hot Shot is worried that the fighting is awakening Unicron from the dead.

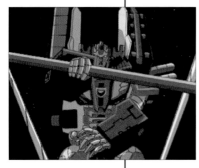

Galvatron wields a metal pole, using it like a sword to fight his enemy, Optimus.

Optimus had to assess the situation quickly.

"I'll take care of Galvatron," ordered Optimus. "You lead the men and attack Unicron with everything you've got!"

Hot Shot didn't need telling twice and ordered an immediate all-out attack on Unicron.

Back on Unicron's surface, Galvatron tore loose a metal pole and used it as a sword to attack Optimus, forcing him to retreat. Optimus took blow after blow, but finally he dodged around the weapon and landed a devastating drop kick on Galvatron.

World at war
The Autobot-Decepticon war began over four million years ago. It started with the struggle to conquer Cybertron, but eventually the conflict stretched across the entire cosmos.

Optimus launches one last ferocious attack on Galvatron.

The two warriors collapsed onto the floor. The mighty Galvatron was mortally wounded.

"You defeated me fair and square," said Galvatron.

Galvatron lies wounded by Optimus's kick.

"No, Galvatron, I think we'll call this one a draw…" offered Optimus, still hopeful of making peace.

"You have to admit," gasped Galvatron, "we're very evenly matched. You know, I've enjoyed every second of our battles, Optimus."

Just as Galvatron finished speaking, the entire structure of Unicron shook. The battle had woken up the planet-eater.

The last battle? Had Galvatron and Optimus Prime become so used to fighting each other that they couldn't imagine a future without their war?

43

Unicron's power feeds on hate. When there is peace, he can no longer live.

Energon
Energon is a type of energy used by both the Transformers and Unicron. Raw Energon is usually found under the surface of planets.

Even though Optimus tries to save him, Galvatron plunges to his death. His sacrifice ends the war.

Deep within Unicron's interior, his heart started beating. The evil one was coming to life again.

His chest unit suddenly opened and began sucking in anything within range.

Optimus Prime grabbed hold of Galvatron just in time to stop him being sucked inside. It took all of Optimus's remaining strength.

"Hang on!" shouted Optimus.

"Why are you saving me, Prime? Let me go, and the war between us will be over," said Galvatron. "Then Unicron will cease to exist!"

Unicron implodes, so that there is no trace that he ever existed.

Optimus refused to drop Galvatron to his doom, but the Decepticon leader had other ideas.

"I said cut me loose, Optimus!" shouted Galvatron.

Galvatron blasted Optimus's arm at point-blank range, making the Autobot let go.

Optimus Prime could only watch helplessly as his enemy Galvatron fell to his death.

With the fighting finally over, Unicron's physical body suddenly had nothing to feed upon.

The evil Unicron flashed out of existence piece by piece—leaving behind an empty void. The battle-scarred body of Optimus Prime was sent hurtling away into deep space, perhaps lost forever…

Powerful energy
Energon is not just sought after by the robot Transformers— other powers in the cosmos, such as the deadly Terrorcons, also desire its power.

Peaceful planet
Learning the terrible truth that Unicron was feeding on the hate generated by their war has made all Transformers promise to work together to rebuild their home world.

After millions of years, the war between the Autobots and the Decepticons was finally over. Without the hatred between the two sides, there was no evil to feed Unicron, and he had faded into nothing.

There was much damage to be repaired, and the Transformers set about rebuilding their shattered home planet of Cybertron, this time living in peace with each other and with the Mini-Cons.

For Rad and his friends, it was time to go home.

"Hey, thanks a lot for the lift guys!" said Rad to Hot Shot and Jetfire. One quick warp-gate journey later, and the kids were back on Earth saying goodbye.

"We'll never forget you," said Carlos, trying to hide the fact that his eyes were far from dry.

"Same here," said Hot Shot. "Thanks, kids, for everything."

"I hope you find Optimus," said Rad.

"The best thing we can do for him," said Hot Shot, "is to make sure that this time the Transformers really do live in peace…"

Lost leader
Optimus Prime is adrift in deep space, but surely the Transformers' search parties will rescue their leader before long?

Hot Shot and Jetfire take the kids back to Earth. They are glad the war is finally over, but it is sad to say goodbye.

The future
When Rad and Carlos grow up they will help the Transformers harvest Energon in a Universe where humans and Transformers work together to explore the cosmos.

Glossary

Allies
People on the same side in a war.

Annihilation
Complete destruction.

Barrage
Continued firing of weapons.

Cell
The smallest unit of a living thing.

Chaos
Complete confusion and disorder.

Consciousness
To be aware of what is going on around you.

Consume
To use something up.

Crave
To want something very much.

Devastating
Causing great destruction.

Dilemma
A difficult choice.

Electricity
A form of energy created by moving particles.

Energy
The power needed to do something.

Engage
To be involved with.

Eons
A very long period of time, such as a thousand million years.

Existence
The state of being alive.

Flagship
The most important ship in a fleet, used by the commanding officers.

Frenzy
Uncontrolled excitement.

Galaxy
A group of billions of stars held together by gravity. Our galaxy is the Milky Way.

Goliath
Large in size.

Hibernation
To spend time in a sleeping state, usually during winter.

Hurtling
Moving at great speed.

Implode
To collapse violently inwards.

Intensify
To make something stronger or more serious.

Materialize
Appear out of nowhere.

Maturity
To behave in an adult manner.

Mercenary
A person who is paid for fighting.

Mercy
Kind treament of an opponent.

Mind
The part of the brain where thoughts and ideas come from.

Moon
A natural body that orbits a planet, such as the Moon around Earth.

A mortal wound
An injury likely to cause death.

Nuclear energy
Power released by changing the atoms of certain chemcials.

Pod
A small vessel.

Range
How far something can travel.

Sacrifice
To give up something for someone or for a special reason.

Traitor
Someone who betrays those close to him or her.

Vortex
A whirling movement, such as the movement of water in a whirlpool.